LIVING WELL

The Art of Making the Best of It

A Little Book about Relating

Michael J Spyker

AgapeDeum

Published in Adelaide, Australia by AgapeDeum
Contact: agapedeum.com

ISBN 978-0-6488957-7-0

Publication assistance by Immortalise

Cover design: Ben Morton

CONTENT

1

Artful Living

Everyone's life is like a painting in development over time. What it will look like depends on many factors. Personality comes into play as do circumstances. So do disposition and personal choices made. What a life's painting finally comes to look like will ever remain an open question. Influencing the process is however possible and necessary.

An actual artist using brush and paint on canvas has a major say on how a scene will be depicted. Inspiration and technique are the key for something special to come about. A competent artist has been willing to learn the craft of painting through commitment and persistence. That is a prerequisite of good art. Most important though is the deeper sensibilities of the artist. The ability of having a unique insight and to respond to what confronts. Also the spontaneity to express that pictorially. No two artists are fully alike.

Living well has similar dynamics in play. In living life every person is an artist. Ideas are shaped by heredity and also upbringing while success requires skill and application. It makes everyone unique. Nothing in life is cut-and-dried with the unpredictable always around the corner. Life is a learning process.

The suggestion that living is a kind of art is far from new. I merely use the idea to highlight the esoteric side of personhood. Life is dictated by deep feelings which can override the cognitive. Like the motivations found within an artist. But in art there are basic rules to be followed. Likewise in life there are principles in play that bring about the best. The question then is, what are these principles and do they even exist?

It has interested me for years: What are the rules for everyone regardless of creed and culture whereby to know that life is lived well? I feel to have found a few rules and of course there will be others. The particular aspect of my insights is that they are anchored into the relational. Modern science recognises that in essence everything exists in relation. People surely do and using relationality as a focus in addressing quality of life makes sense. Bill Bryson in his book *The Body* notes that frequent, quality relating with significant others lengthens the telomeres in our DNA, which in old age reduces the chance of illness and thus death (p. 437).

By nature people are spirited beings. I have sought to understand it from a Christian spirituality perspective and have written about it using insights from other disciplines as well e.g. philosophy, psychology and science. Much of those studies involved the relational. This time I will present my findings without religious or academic terminology. The information will be concise and easy to understand. It will also be practical. Its validity is for the reader to decide. Life experience and common sense will easily suffice in making an evaluation.

I would not write any of what is to come unless my wife and I had practised it and seen its benefits. Ask our five children and they will tell that as a parents we have made mistakes. Perfection is not possible. 'Good enough' will do fine. Also, life is a process. Mistakes are to be learned from and curve balls are ever flying in as a further test.

Living Well addresses the importance of disposition and persistence. It invites to being a certain kind of person and how to get there. Someone good to be with and competent across the relational spectrum: from family to friends, work or in the pub. By all means add this little book to the self-help category. *Living Well* reaches deeply into the psyche with ideas that are deceptively ordinary. It touches the essential being of the artist of life and offers ways in which to paint a picture of beauty.

2

Wellbeing of Soul

Personhood is a complex phenomenon that everyone is inescapably confronted with. As a person I have that sense of living within a body but also somehow being extended beyond it. Generally this is referred to by saying that people have a spirit or, as some prefer to call it, a soul. In either case, it points to the deeper side of human nature, that which reaches into the sub-conscious. I prefer the term spirit for the consciously unknown and hold that soul involves awareness. That approach allows for a more nuanced discussion about the various levels of human experience, which for our present purposes is mostly irrelevant. In whatever way you wish to explain it, people are deep waters.

Always human experience is a relational event. When I look at a tree it is an encounter of my senses and an interpretation of that with my mind. The tree and I do exist in relation. It becomes much more interesting when interacting with an animal and further so when meeting another human being. While the most difficult person to relate to is myself, which is a 24/7 experience. The relational is inescapable in life and determines its quality to quite a large extent. When interactions are relationally okay, life has a solid base to build on. When otherwise, there is that crumbling feeling. Of all dynamics involved in being alive, the relational determines most with regard to the wellbeing of soul. Or, as I would prefer to describe it, the wellbeing of my spirit. Relation is an expression of that which is deepest within me – of spirit. About spirituality I hold that its quality is firstly determined by the nature of a person's relationality with expressions of religion and other 'spirit' focused activities being a possible add-on.

Of course, there are skills to be learned in relating well – or possibly deviously. It involves techniques, which are a matter of communication. Much more significant is the underlying nature of the relational intent, un-modified by skilled expression. The true quality of an interaction derives from a person's disposition. Good fruit does not grow on an average tree. My inclination towards others matters. There are many aspects to disposition, personality traits being one of them. Some people are generous by nature and some stingy. There are introverts and extroverts, risk takers and cautious folk. Whatever the make-up of an individual, relational intent can be adjusted towards what is wise and good, rather what is questionable. It is the key to living well.

I am convinced that seeking to relate from an informed basis is the best thing that can happen to a person. It solidifies identity for I will know deep down what I am about and the value of it. I have been criticised in life much like everyone else. I have been misunderstood or ignored. I have made mistakes. Hurts have come my way, some quite painful. But I have not let that shake me. My self-worth has not thus been diminished. Not because I proudly declare myself worthy. Rather, I have made good relational principles the benchmark of my behaviour whatever it takes. It has become the measure of my worth and it is a private assessment.

Society has all kinds of ways whereby to measure success, most of it a mirage. I have my own take on that. Whatever a person's accomplishments, dubious relational intent means coming up short.

Fortunately, the relational principles to be suggested are few and readily understood. They are intrinsic to human nature and make sense. Competent relating strengthens personhood – my own and that of those I am in contact with. Family life will improve as will other situations.

Thus far, I have tried to establish the priority of relating above whatever else has value in life. It is now time to present my relational frame of reference.

3

Place-making

Many years ago Paul Tournier, a Swiss doctor and psychologist, was told by a troubled student that he was always looking for a place. The student had been richly provided for in growing up but suffered the outcomes of absentee parenting. Tournier understood that the young man suffered from a lack of real belonging and decided that this lack would forever lead him on a search for a sense of place somewhere – most likely without much success. On the positive side Tournier concluded that when someone did have a good sense of place psychologically, then that person could take that sense anywhere and would be able to live feeling grounded. The troubled student had grown up emotionally disenfranchised in spite of a well-meant luxurious childhood. The story highlights the fundamental significance of the relational in life;

how important it is to get it right. People need places.

Reflecting on this, I constructed a simple visualisation involving four concepts that explains what good place-making is about. An idea that is practical and readily remembered.

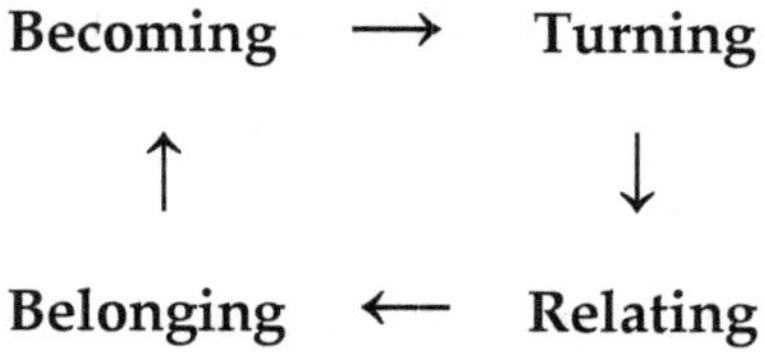

When these four concepts interact well, it means that personal wholeness becomes possible. It happens over time. The cornerstone of place-making is belonging because without a sense of belonging the other three factors will struggle in finding their potential. The concepts involve the following.

Belonging means finding a place of acceptance, at its best unconditionally.

Becoming involves personal growth and depends on the nature of belonging for its quality.

Turning means being inclined towards the demands of a healthy belonging.

Relating allows for turning to be communicated to facilitate a bonding.

Creating a place of nurture starts with *belonging,* which then facilitates a *becoming.* The person being nurtured must *turn* towards those dynamics and communicate positively through *relating.* This relating will enhance the sense of belonging and the circular movement of the equation starts all over again.

The four dynamics work anti-clockwise as well. A feeling of belonging will make relating easier, which improves the readiness of turning towards, rather than away. That helps with growing into one's place and improves the sense of belonging.

For place-making to be effective each factor must function adequately and a weak link undermines its overall potential. Place-making is dynamic and varied as a process. Outcomes are achieved over time. In short – stay with it!

The place-making equation applies to all interpersonal situations. That includes groups like family, at work or in community. Society is well aware of the need for people to belong. The predominant reference for this is the use of the word family – like the football family. A sports club invites me into its *belonging* embrace and urges me towards *becoming* a member.   I may legitimately tap into the club's history which is an identity enhancer. But club membership has its demands. It is expected that I will be *turning* my hand towards matters that need looking after and my wallet towards the club's financial needs. I must be interactive and *relate* with fellow supporters to create a special bond. Then my sense of *belonging* will become strengthened. In that way I will find my place of recognition within the club. That sense of place may become challenged when the club experiences internal difficulties. If my feelings of belonging weather the disagreements, I will remain. If not, I may begin to seek a place elsewhere. This loss of place can be traumatic depending on how deeply my belonging is felt.

One aspect of the place-making concept still needs a mention. The left side of *belonging* and *becoming* is mostly passive. A place of *belonging* is psychologically *provided by others*. I cannot make it happen on my own. This passivity applies to *becoming* as well. Without a real sense of belonging, any becoming into wholeness will be limited. The situation of Tournier's student makes that clear.

The right side, of *turning* and *relating*, is *active and under my control*. I must *turn* towards my situational environment, if it is a good one, and *relate* rather than withdraw to strengthen my wellbeing. It is my choice.

The task of good place-makers is twofold. They should be sufficient at place-making themselves and must help others develop likewise. That is particularly relevant to a parenting role. More will be said about that later.

Place-making is not easy but very worthwhile. It helps that the four concepts involved may be readily remembered. Common sense supports their validity. As a frame of reference for behaviour it ticks many boxes.

4

Interlude

Our modern world suffers from an overdose of information. It comes quickly and is unrelenting. Seek out any topic and with the click of a mouse varied opinions will appear. In many ways this can be helpful in others it is not. With so many ideas around, how is their validity properly measured? Mostly it is not and suggestions are taken on board according to personal preference. It is often lightly held and will soon change when a seemingly better idea arrives. Being convinced of something significant and sticking to it has become uncommon. Not that a change of mind is necessarily a bad idea. But how well informed is that change?

It is also true that for many people information has become an entertainment of sorts. The media and its ever present influences are a clear sign of that. Self-help books often fit that category. Valuable ideas are well presented and create a feel-good factor. It's fine. Publishers will seek to make their books attractive thus facilitating sales. The entertaining aspect may translate it into a comfort zone, you enjoy the read, think it rather good, but then soon move on to the next book without internalising information that could change life for the better. The reading itself lacks an assimilation process sufficient in making a permanent difference.

The little book *Living Well* offers neither feel-good nor in-depth explanations. It holds that what is valuable, when easy to understand and remembered, will stick into the mind best through a simple and focused presentation. Much depends on the response of the reader. Information that appeals may be well worth revisiting and internalising. Simplicity makes that easier. When an idea fails to resonate, no secondary information or anecdote will change that. In scientific theory there is the concept of an elegant solution. It believes that simple insights have the best chance of success. There must be proof of their validity of course.

Life cannot be built wisely on an oversupply of data. I decided to search for what really matters years ago. For ideas that stand the test of time and seem to be of significance to personhood overall. As mentioned, I settled on the relational as most important. What I am presenting are my findings in a nutshell, the kernel of my focus in life with all else being significant but secondary. And there is a great deal of that which many experiences have taught me. I enjoy a personal library of books across the major disciplines. I negotiate all that in the knowledge that deep down the real value of my life rests not in books but on a few core relational principles I seek to adhere to. Knowledge is helpful but it will not define my identity. In my view, it is always the relational that determines someone's stature. It is a competency that can be learned.

Hopefully, as you continue reading, the picture will achieve further clarity. In the next chapter a relational model is presented that feeds directly into the place-making concept. I have discussed its design with a professor of psychology who confirmed its validity. The basics appeal to common sense which facilitates the model's effectiveness. It explains how to develop and direct inner motivations towards the wellbeing of self and others. A good model seeks to make accessible that which in reality is complex and interwoven, by using simple ideas. Like the thought that personhood involves body, soul and spirit, while an actual person is indivisible. A model is to offer a frame of reference for improved understanding. I trust that my relational model resonates with how you feel life should be best lived. If so, please make sure to make the ideas your own, which is best achieved through practice.

5

A Model of Relating

People are capable of both the good and the bad and they know it. This ability is called morality, a fully relational phenomenon. The good and the bad are a helpful demarcation when seeking to understand how relationality works in its deepest motivations. They play out unavoidably within every person.

I suggest there to be three primary dynamics in play for either side. They function in opposition and the question is which side will have the upper-hand. If it is the good, then life will be psychologically healthy. When the bad side rules, wellbeing will disintegrate. Fortunately, by knowing what is happening within myself and the choices I can make, the good may disempower what is bad. Focus on what is relationally healthy and the negative fades into the background.

But it will never disappear and it is always ready to strike.

Relational self-assessment is key to really living well. Invariably in my motivation and behaviour I express a relational mix of good and bad. How to interpret that is best explained in the form of a model. In its simplest presentation it will appear at the end of this chapter. For the full model please refer to chapters 9 and 10. So, let's have a look.

What is the overall disposition of the good and the bad like? That of good I would classify as a *loving interest*. Loving not solely in a significant emotional sense but also in that of charity. While the disposition of the bad side is one of *egotistic disinterest*. Clearly the two are antagonistic, which is central to how the model works.

For each side, for the good and the bad, there are three *Primary Expressions* that dictate what relating will be like. On the positive side these three are *Care*, applying *Responsibility* and having *Integrity*. Together they will encourage and nurture wellbeing, both emotionally and physically. The opposing three expressions are *Oppression, Neglect* and *Manipulation.* They have a demoralising effect which results in the disintegration of personhood, away from what would be beneficial.

The *Primary Expressions* just mentioned each lead to a final *Outcome* by a number of intermediate steps. Those steps, explained in chapter 9, will not be discussed as yet. *Primary Expression* and *Outcome* will suffice in understanding what relating is essentially about. It works as follows.

Relational *Outcomes* are formed within each person *over time* and depend on the kind of relating someone has been exposed to. When experiencing the *Primary Expression* of 'Care' it will help a recipient in being able to care also. It shapes a person into being willing to have *compassion*, which is its *Outcome.* While the *Primary Expression* of 'Responsibility', with people who take their role seriously, creates within the recipient a sense of *personal freedom.* They will learn to live within responsible boundaries. Freedom, not in the form of doing as you please, but rather in that of becoming what you should become. And thirdly, exposure to honesty, which involves the *Primary Expression* of 'Integrity', fosters *wholeness*, an integration of identity. You will have confidence in who you are as a person and will not be readily shaken. Compassion, Freedom and Wholeness are the three *Outcomes* of relating towards 'the good.'

The negative side of relating concerns 'Oppression' with *rebellion* as a consequence. In desperation the recipient will begin to fight back behaviourally, not just against the oppressor but potentially society also. 'Neglect' has a similar effect, that of *anarchy*. If you don't care about me, why should I care about anything – not even myself. While 'Manipulation' leads to inner *weakness*, the fragmentation of identity. Manipulation involves emotional blackmail with dire consequences. Rebellion, Anarchy and Weakness are the *Outcomes* of relating towards 'the bad.'

If you find this too brief an explanation please read chapter 9 in which further detail is given. My present aim is towards a concise formulation of the most important aspects of relating suitable as a reference for easy memorisation.

The Good

Characteristic:

Loving Interest

The Bad

Characteristic:

Egotistic Disinterest

Expression / Outcome

Care	*Compassion*
Responsibility	*Freedom*
Integrity	*Wholeness*

Expression / Outcome

Oppression	*Rebellion*
Neglect	*Anarchy*
Manipulation	*Weakness*

Focus on the positive and the negative will thereby be minimised. If it seems a lot to remember, please accept that it is not that difficult. After a while the ideas will settle nicely into the mind. That is what happened to me. So once in a while I have a look at the full model as well to refresh my understanding (Chapter 10). It may point out matters I could work at that are not mentioned above.

6

Walking Around

Living Well is a little book that informs what basically relating is about. It is an all-of-person activity that never stops. If the information has kept your interest thus far, it shows your affinity with the topic. With something as complex as the relational, a complete mastery of it is impossible. Neither is it necessary. A little good, however imperfectly expressed, will go a long way. Taking the model's ideas on board will be easier when you are naturally inclined towards the good, which most people are. Being aware of the negative side of relating is helpful in knowing what to avoid, within yourself and with interactions that come your way from other people.

Of course, I make mistakes many a time. Most are little hick-ups but some have been more troublesome. Those

I will always remember and regret. Such is life and the memories keep me humble. I will not let the situation become an emotional self-hurt. For I mean well and I am only human. I will take care not to misstep in the same manner – hopefully.

Years ago an interesting question came my way: 'How much space do you feel you have, walking around within yourself?' It is a quite deeply penetrating idea. What freedom do I experience within my spirit, or do I feel restricted by memories and self-accusations? It takes confidence to be free. It also takes an approach that doesn't do self-pity. So how will I make sure to relate well towards myself? In this the relational model is a help.

Positive psychology has become popular. Its focus is on beneficial possibilities and opportunities towards positive change. It accepts that this is never easy and demands character. Addressing the relational in life requires exactly the same approach. With the proviso that deep-seated emotional infections in the soul do not disappear simply by being positive. It may need specialised attention and perhaps can never be fully healed. Nevertheless, even when suffering in this way an ability to focus on the positive will have its benefits. Some people with significant psychological hurts have done incredible well.

How then do I walk around relationally within myself? Always I try to stay positive and cut myself some slack. I don't do perfection and practise kindness towards my own soul as an act of *caring*. Though *responsible* for my own behaviour I will not become a disciplinarian towards myself. But I won't shun the hard yards where needed. Good food, enough exercise and sleep all are important to me. It takes effort to make that happen. Finally, I will not tell myself a lie and seek to *honestly* bell the cat. There is no point in fooling my own mind for it will only undermine my self-respect.

Such self-conditioning makes good relating towards others easier. After all, I will be projecting that which I am well familiar with within myself. It is summed up by six questions about positive relating that I should keep in mind.

1. Is my thinking affirmative?
2. Am I willing to care?
3. Do I have a role to play?
4. Am I acting responsibly?
5. Am I showing integrity?
6. How about respect?

Walking around within myself may be difficult when something is bothering me. A superficial bother I tend to shrug my shoulders at. It will pass. A bother that comes from deep within my unconscious I will reflect on, not necessarily finding an answer. I accept it and will seek to limit the emotional attention it demands thus safeguarding my inner freedom. If there is an answer, I will attend to it positively always with the relational principles in mind. In that way I try to keep my life on track towards psycho-spiritual health.

Please accept that I do not for a moment suggest this to be easy. People have different approaches to dealing with problems and that is appreciated. I dare say that in every case relational principles will be relevant which is helpful to know.

7

Partner and Parent

It will have become quite obvious that good relating involves being other-centred. No surprises there. It is particularly important when living with a partner and a family. Tounier's student was an example of how things can go wrong. A positive attitude is necessary not just towards myself but very much also in keeping a keen eye upon the needs of others. I must always be ready to modify my behaviour when it steers towards the questionable and remain aware of how easily that might happen. Fortunately, with Care, Responsibility and Integrity as my modus operandi I tend to notice the negative readily for it is not my disposition.

Negative relational interactions are demoralising and nobody fully escapes them. Inevitably so in intimate relationships. Some behavioural mistakes I am extra watchful of, such as being careful not to disrespect the vulnerabilities of my partner. I will not verbally hit below the belt. Words can be damaging and people are far more sensitive than is generally perceived. Not that I will not ever speak my mind. Caring never means becoming a doormat. I may agree to disagree and have opinions. Those are not set in concrete with change always a possibility that will happen with good reason.

The negative in relating leads to dire consequences. Children in particular are in need of a safe relational environment for it will affect them for life. Family dynamics will leave a relational imprint on a child in accordance with the dominant relational factors being exposed to. It starts at birth and will continue to have its effects ever after.

There are three negative behaviours to be avoided. Firstly, I must not be overly authoritarian or *dictatorial.* Overly, because there are boundaries to be set that are beneficial to child development. It is best done with the inclusion of an explanation even when a child may not understand it. Arbitrariness is a no-no and with older children in particular. Neither must I ever *withdraw* from my responsibilities emotionally and practically. Such parental neglect leaves children adrift without a sufficient sense of security. From Tournier's student we may learn that providing well materially is not enough. Parenthood of quality involves an emotional investment that is uniquely personal between the parent and the child.

That leaves the third behavioural mistake I must avoid. It is an important one and often not recognised for its seriousness. I should always avoid *emotional blackmail*. The key word here is manipulation, which is different from promising a reward for a task that is well done. Manipulation seeks to achieve things by undermining a person emotionally. Like: 'You are such a good boy, I'm sure you will help me.' Or, 'If you don't help me, I'm not sure about tomorrow's ballgame.' Rather, be upfront with: 'How about I help you and you help me? I take you to the ballgame tomorrow and you help me in the garden today.' The two approaches are quite different. One plays the emotions by alluding to a measuring up, while the other is a simple, matter of fact proposition and thus cognitive.

A child has no effective responses to manipulation. It is an easy habit for a parent to slip into and perhaps not seen for what it is. People can be manipulative without being aware of it. Parents projecting their own desires strongly upon their children is manipulative. Manipulation compels emotionally and disempowers.

Having been exposed to manipulation at work I used the following tactic in countering it. First of all, in my mind I would call the interaction for what it was. I would remain in charge mentally and not buy into the manipulative approach. Next, I would decide on how to respond. I might act as requested, but only because it was I alone who decided so. Thus I took control over the manipulation. At all times my decision would be unemotional and protect my self-worth and integrity.

Manipulation involves a meta-message – an unspoken expectation that is value laden. As a partner and parent I have to be very careful here. Coercion is out of place in good relating. I know for a certainty that if I were to address my wife manipulatively, she would pull me up on it right away, which is great. We take relating seriously. When children are exposed to manipulation consistently, it prevents the developing of their inner strength. Their measuring up to expectation is being questioned and they never feel their worth to be an absolute certainty, which keeps them ever dependent. Talking about sad!

8

Finding My Place

Life is complex and so am I. Not ever will I fully understand myself. With other people it is only of those close to me that I have some idea what makes them tick. Fortunately, the six relational principles function regardless of all that. I consider them to be generic – applicable to every person. The principles accommodate cultural differentiation. Societal norms may differ but the basics of good relating remain the same.

Many a serious problem in life involves a violation of positive relating with the negative being dominant. That is so at a personal and family level as well as a societal one. It even applies with regard to nature. Mistreat our world and matters will deteriorate. Climate change is a case in point.

I create my particular place within my world. A place that is determined by who I consider myself to be. It involves a willingness to improve my disposition. That will take time with the benefits possibly well down the road. The relational is always a slow growing fruit. Many of its influences I may never know about and don't need to. Throw a little love around, the saying goes. People will be blessed by it and with that focus life will be worth living.

Positive relational influences are always helpful and paramount in assisting children and young people to develop well. But the relational alone is not enough. Knowledge about stages of personal developments also will come in handy. In fact, it is this that started my search for insights into the relational, now decades ago. I was teaching the stages of growth in children to a group of parents when it occurred to me that an ability to evaluate their own disposition would be beneficial. For it always colours behaviour and surely towards their children even though parents may not be aware of this. Upon reflection I realised that the key to such an evaluation would be an understanding of the relational. Thus the *Living Well* model was created.

Some knowledge of human development from birth till old age is helpful. This field of psychology has been studied extensively. I would like to mention a few ideas to keep in mind. The life periods mentioned are flexible and may differ somewhat per individual. In modern society, with the young being well cared for, physical development tends to happen faster while the psychological side may be delayed.

STAGES OF GROWTH

Babies They need unconditional nurture, much body contact and the security of sheltered dependence.

Pre-School Children must feel free to explore in an environment of loving discipline. Becoming used to boundaries will help them find freedom within that. The boundaries must be established kindly and not be gender specific.

Primary School Children must be helped in character development. Values and skills are taught diligently and with patience. Easy success is not helpful for a child, nor is not being praised for a task well done or showing a good attitude.

High School   Teenagers must feel appreciated and expect to be treated by parents as equals. Individuation becomes a serious challenge with many a hick-up and frustration. Parents must be patient during this process and cut the teenager some slack within reason. Always choose your battles. When well-loved and accepted the young person will end up okay. Being aware of his or her personality type will be helpful as well.

Young Adult   They must stand on their own two feet, have the courage of independence and be allowed to follow their own star. Parents must step back and not project their ideas and anxieties upon the young adult. Good advice, however, never goes astray when wise and open-minded. With young adulthood a search for meaning arises, posing the question of 'Who am I?' It will follow the young adult for years to come.

Later Adult   (from 40-50 onwards) A period of settling down with more time available for (significant) others. It becomes accepted that 'No man is an island.' Success is appreciated but tempered by the need for friends. In a mature life people are valued above the material. 'It is your influences that will outlast you. Make them good ones.' It's what a friend of mine was told by his father.

It is very brief but these insight about growing up have helped me. In the next chapters the relational model is fully explained. It is followed by 'Wilson Road', 12 interesting stories that feature relational principles in a family situation. Just a bit of serious fun.

In writing all this I feel to have presented myself in a better light that reality might support. The canvas of my life has a fair few darker spots on it. But overall it looks okay, which I ascribe to having discovered the relational principles. Living is indeed an art and my painting is not finished. I will keep trying to brighten it up, make the best of it. Thank you for reading on to this point.

9

Working the Relational Model

Place-making is central to a healthy psychological development. With it being fully relational, success will depend on which interactive dynamics have the upper hand. The *Living Well Model of Relating* suggests three positive dynamics called *Motivators*, with three *Demoralisers* as their negative, opposing forces. The *Primary Expression* and *Outcome* for each dynamic have already been discussed offering basic insights on how relating works.

A further understanding of *Motivators* and *Demoralisers* becomes possible by recognising *Seven Factors* that will be readily understood as words are used common to everyday conversation. How these factors are named and their specific influences needs an explanation. If at first this may seem complex, please dig in a little and the conceptualisation will become clearer.

An explanation is best discussed by using a primary dynamic and address its importance in detail. For this I have selected *Motivator 2*. The full model is presented in the next chapter and you might quickly familiarise yourself with its structure. It will help in understanding what I am to explain. It should not be overly difficult to apply the approach taken with *Motivator 2* to the other five relational principles.

The Seven Factors of a Relational Dynamic
They are separate but interwoven

Factor 1 is called *Fundamental Orientation*.

It is the overall intent of a primary relational dynamic. For *Motivator 2* that intent is the use of **Authority,** which is not a popular word these days because of its negative connotations. However, without there being authority the world would run riot as would family life. The right kind of authority will work towards the wellbeing of others or, when dealing with my private thoughts and emotions, that of myself.

Factor 2 is called *Primary Expression.*

For *Motivator 2* it means that authority always involves ***Responsibility*** for it to be safe. I must be responsible with the needs and wellbeing of others and myself. Primary Expression is an action word that connects with the Fundamental Orientation.

Factor 3 is called *Technique.*

This factor describes how the purpose of a Primary Expression becomes best realised and what kind of relational atmosphere will be created. For *Motivator 2* that means instilling ***Discipline***. The three Motivators always interact, which in positive relating means that discipline will be tempered by care and openness. But encouragement to adhere to set rules is needed for a healthy personal development.

Factor 4 is called *Relational Interaction.*

This factor shows why the Technique is relevant. For *Motivator 2* it transmits the desire that those under discipline will thus become ***Enabled*** and encouraged towards maturity. An undisciplined life is destined for disaster.

Factor 5 is called *Basic Attitude*.

It is an important factor in relating, inseparable from Technique and Relational Interaction, and determines much. For *Motivator* 2 the Basic Attitude should be that of **Dependability.** It signifies that I can be counted on as the one in authority but in turn expect that from those in my care.

Factor 6 is called *Existential Reality*.

It depicts what kind of place (environment) is available to those under my authority. The sense of this place affects people on 'the inside'. The Existential Reality is shaped by the previous five factors together and much determines the Primary Outcome. For *Motivator* 2 this Existential Reality should convey that an **Opportunity** is available to me towards becoming my own person when practising the discipline of self-control.

Factor 7 is called *Primary Outcome*.

The Primary Outcome is the long-term psychological effect when being consistently exposed to a relational dynamic. When living under positive authority I would have learned to keep myself in check where needed and thus may enjoy a true sense of **Freedom**. My mentor (the one with authority over me) will have shown the way towards liberty of person within the boundaries of wisdom. It is a much needed aspect in leaving a beneficial relational imprint upon my life.

A way of using the above would be by remembering the terms written in bold/italic. Aim for those and you will do well. Their significance can be summed up in one sentence for easy reference. For *Motivators 2* the sentence reads as follows.

> *Authority* involves *Responsibility* and uses *Discipline* to *Enable* based on a *Dependability* that offers *Opportunity* towards *Freedom*.

At the end of the next chapter the sentences for the other five relational principles may be found.

10

Living Well

Model of Relating

ABOUT THE GOOD

An insight that resonates

Is to be enjoyed,

And its price to be paid.

MOTIVATOR 1

1. *Fundamental Orientation*
Love
I will think favourably of others and be merciful.

2. *Primary Expression*
Care
I will provide for and watch over.

3. *Technique*
Kindness
I will be patient and forgiving.

4. *Relational Interaction*
Understanding
I will be humble and remember my vulnerability.

5. *Basic Attitude*
Other-centeredness
I have empathy and desire to be of help.

6. *Existential Reality*
Personal Development
I am committed to your identity formation.

7. *Primary Outcome*
Compassion
I will encourage you to care for others as you yourself wish to be cared for.

MOTIVATOR 2

1. *Fundamental Orientation*
   Authority
   I will work towards the wellbeing of others and myself.

2. *Primary Expression*
   Responsibility
   I will respond to the needs of others.

3. *Technique*
   Discipline
   I will expect right application and restraint.

4. *Relational Interaction*
   Enabling
   I will encourage maturity.

5. *Basic Attitude*
   Dependability
   I will see matters through.

6. *Existential Reality*
   Opportunity
   It will encourage self-control.

7. *Primary Outcome*
   Freedom
   I will show you the way of personal liberty within the boundaries of wisdom.

MOTIVATOR 3

1. *Fundamental Orientation*
   Harmony
   I will seek harmony where no ethical and moral principles are at stake.

2. *Primary Expression*
   Integrity
   I will practise what I preach.

3. *Technique*
   Consistency
   I will not be unpredictable in attitude and behaviour.

4. *Relational Interaction*
   Appreciation
   I will show you respect.

5. *Basic Attitude*
   Honesty
   I will practise openness.

6. *Existential Reality*
   Support
   I seek to travel roads together.

7. *Primary Outcome*
   Wholeness
   I will help you in finding an integrated personality.

DEMORALISER 1

1. *Fundamental Orientation*
   Dictatorship
   I will have my way with little regard for others.

2. *Primary Expression*
   Oppression
   I am the enforcer of issues.

3. *Technique*
   Rule
   My demands will be met.

4. *Relational Interaction*
   Compliance
   I do not accept objections.

5. *Basic Attitude*
   Dominance
   You will succumb.

6. *Existential Reality*
   Confinement
   I can overpower you.

7. *Primary Outcome*
   Rebellion
   Your anger does not concern me.

DEMORALISER 2

1. *Fundamental Orientation*
    Desertion
    I refuse being responsible.

2. *Primary Expression*
    Neglect
    I can turn my back on you.

3. *Technique*
    License
    I leave you to your choices.

4. *Relational Interaction*
    Being left at bay
    I will not protect you.

5. *Basic Attitude*
    Irresponsibility
    I do not value you.

6. *Existential Reality*
    Abandonment
    I will not be found.

7. *Primary Outcome*
    Anarchy
    Destructiveness is not my worry.

DEMORALISER 3

1. *Fundamental Orientation*
    Disharmony
    I do not seek companionship.

2. *Primary Expression*
    Manipulation
    I will emotionally misuse you.

3. *Technique*
    Lure
    I will draw you in underhandedly.

4. *Relational Interaction*
    Appeasement
    I will set you to my personal advantage.

5. *Basic Attitude*
    Coercion
    I will pressure and persuade you.

6. *Existential Reality*
    Blackmail
    I will exploit your emotions and fears.

7. *Primary Outcome*
    Weakness
    Your vulnerability and disintegration do not concern me.

Quick Glance Reference

Motivator 1

> *Love* involves *Care* and uses *Kindness* showing *Understanding* based on an *Other-centeredness* that helps *Personal Development* towards *Compassion*.

Motivator 2

> *Authority* involves *Responsibility* and uses *Discipline* to *Enable* based on a *Dependability* that offers *Opportunity* towards *Freedom*.

Motivator 3

> *Harmony* involves *Integrity* and uses *Consistency* showing *Appreciation* and *Honesty* in *Support* towards *Wholeness*.

Demoraliser 1

> *Dictatorship* involves *Oppression* and uses *Rules* to enforce *Compliance* projecting *Dominance* and a sense of *Confinement* that leads to *Rebellion*.

Demoraliser 2

> **Desertion** involves **Neglect** that takes **License** to **Leave at Bay** because of **Irresponsibility** which creates **Abandonment** and results in **Anarchy**.

Demoraliser 3

> **Disharmony** involves **Manipulation** and uses **Lure** to achieve **Appeasement** through **Coercion** exploiting emotions with **Blackmail** which results in **Weakness** of identity.

Living well is enhanced by a model of understanding that can be depended on. Whether the relational model fits that bill, you are welcome to decide. It surely has helped me over the years in the art of making the best of life.

Wilson Road

Twelve short stories about relating - about people and family life. Perhaps they make you smile. Each story ends with three questions for reflection. Not to find the right answers necessarily, but to assist in engaging with the relational dynamics found in the story. Why not have a go?

1

A smile with real meaning

Come on, Peter muttered under his breath and pushed the brakes to avoid a bumper touch. I hate this road, he thought. Peter was on his way home from work. It had been a cow of a day. His thoughts weren't exactly on the traffic and this sudden moment of a near miss sharpened his focus – somewhat. He wasn't thinking of work either, though there was plenty to worry about. It was the home front that engaged his mind and feelings: Amelia, and Sarah, and Henry.

Peter loved them, but wondered whether his emotions had flattened out more than would be desirable. Family life seemed hard work. Perhaps he was just tired. For a moment last week an enormous surge of love had come flooding over him to the point of wiping some tears away. Totally surprising that. It had happened unannounced while working in their garden and thinking of his wife. Creative, impulsive Amelia, who could smile a thousand different smiles. Of course, he loved then all. He just couldn't always muster the corresponding feelings in dealing with family stuff – always busy, living side by side, with the usual pressure or friction that made the machinery squeak. Those feelings of love, what actually was that supposed to be about in the daily grind? How could you know if you were doing alright?

And there was the rub. Peter braked harder than normal once more, grateful for driving a modern safe car. Someone cutting in before him without much indication. Forty minutes of getting home through peak traffic. By nature he was an impatient driver and his nerves were on edge when he reached home. It always was good to arrive in their driveway. But sometimes good to escape also.

As parents, they had decided to enrol in a course on relating called *Living Well* lasting a few months. It had been Amelia's idea. Perhaps she felt something was amiss between them though that was not how the matter was raised.

'We can learn,' she had said, 'and it's important. Do it for me and the children.'

'But am I that bad?'

'No, you're fine,' Amelia had smiled. So they went yesterday evening for the first time. It was okay and promised much food for thought. Peter particularly remembered that a good relational motivation makes up for inadequacies. If you are willing to ascribe to some key relational principles, that is. Amelia had been unusually quiet. He realised that the outcome of good relating is wellbeing for yourself and those in your care. Feelings are quite important, but not all. Responding correctly to situations regardless of how you felt would be the default action to fall back on. The relational principles involved were not difficult to understand with ideas that seemed okay and timely, Peter had to admit. Next week would reveal more.

Why does Henry always have to dump his bike in the middle of their small front lawn, Peter thought irritably? One day someone is bound to nick it, he'd told Henry. 'Nah,' Henry answered, with the wisdom of a 10 year old. 'Who'd want it?'

Welcome home Dad, at Wilson Road.

Reflections

- If love isn't a feeling necessarily, how might it be expressed?
- Why might I be reluctant to learn more about relating?
- What is my general attitude to life like?

2

Do I really want to do this?

Amelia had made a fresh coffee and bit into some cake. Perhaps it might cheer her up a little. Not that anything terrible had happened. But keeping her usually happy countenance had become increasingly a struggle of late. I'm simply too complex, she reflected, and felt a shadow drift over her soul. It unnerved her. Getting out of this mood needed a dose of positive thinking. A remedy she had tried often before and, until recently, with considerable success. Seeing the bright side of life was the best way. Unfortunately, today it didn't work.

Sarah, at thirteen, was beginning to compete in the female side of the family in all sorts of little ways. Nothing very major. But being challenged, however insignificantly, was disturbing Amelia. It was not fun. Also, it also needed a wise response, which was easier said than done. Where do you draw the line? What is best overlooked? Which are the benchmarks? Amelia felt out of her depth and was afraid that the fun-loving relationship with her daughter had begun to slip away. 'Life's serious as well, mum,' Sarah had blurted out once. It had left Amelia momentarily speechless. Not because she was unaware of the painful side of life, but her usual response was trying to remain upbeat. Was that the easy way out perhaps? Sarah, unknowingly, had hit a nerve.

Peter was not happy either. Things were getting on top of him. Nothing too drastic, but that confidence in the successes of life was fading. It worried Amelia and affected her like a slowly dripping tap. All of this coming gradually as the relationship with her family was increasingly being tested. Nothing abnormal and no more than what happened in many other families. But it pained Amelia and she had been at a loss in how to respond.

Some months ago, in a moment of clear insight for which she took no credit, she had understood that in all that was happening the relational dynamics in her family should not be taken for granted as being okay. Looking for answers she had come across *Living Well,* a course on relational principles and decided to enrol. Peter had agreed for them to attend together. Dear Peter had known better than to refuse. To his credit, he admitted to sensing the need for what she suggested and was willing to give it a shot. Together, they would work through the information received and be open about it. The first few evenings at *Living Well* had been informative. It encouraged a readiness to accept each other's complexities and personality differences, not to mention those of gender. Plus hidden psychological needs that coloured their relationship. In short, they were trying to become more tolerant of each other. What stood out was the need for a desire to 'want to do this!' They had talked about that one night in bed.

It is so much nicer to avoid all these struggles, Amelia mused, and to live happily. Happily, in denial, it would be. For her the importance of good family dynamics weighed heavily and that helped her to see the course through.

The doorbell rang. No rest for the wicked.

Reflections

- What might be the connections between unhappiness and relating?
- How much might good relating depend on personality type if at all?
- What is smart about not taking relational dynamics for granted?

3

A phone calamity

'Where did you put it, tell me?' Sarah shouted at her brother. 'Where's my phone?'

Henry shrugged his shoulders, unconcerned. 'No idea.'

'Mum, he hid my phone. Tell him to get it.' Sarah turned towards her mother.

'I'll phone it,' Amelia said wanting to resolve the problem quickly.

The phone rang from underneath a cushion. Sarah grabbed it and ran out of the room slamming the door. Peter wearily got up and followed her. Sarah's behaviour of late needed addressing

Walking through the house to her bedroom he remembered to keep his cool with his children. He was getting tired of that bickering though. Sarah needed another talking to. But not like last time. It struck him again how ineffective that had been. Peter stopped in the middle of the passageway to think. After the latest *Living Well* evening, he had decided on being non-judgmental and considerate. Amelia and he had talked it over. It wasn't that difficult relating well, if you managed to remember in time. This time he would not give Sarah a piece of his mind.

'Go away, Dad – please!' Sarah was sitting on her bed. 'You don't understand.'

'I'm not cross, Sarah.'

Sarah looked at her father. Searchingly.

'What is so terrible about a misplaced phone?'

'I needed it,' Sarah said angrily.

'May I say something please?' Peter asked. Sarah shrugged her shoulders.

'Mum and I like to help you. Therefore we happily pay for the cost of your phone. But there is no need to make such a fuss if you cannot immediately find it.'

'But Henry hid it – on purpose,' Sarah retorted.

'Yes, I believe he might have. That's wrong and I'll sort it,' Peter promised. 'But, you have your own ways of annoying him on purpose too.'

'It's still wrong.'

'So, it's not wrong to stomp out of the room slamming the door?'

'That's different – it's emotional.'

'Ah – so if I had stormed in here and emotionally gave you a verbal hiding, it would have been okay?'

Sarah didn't respond. Dad was right of course, but it didn't help much.

'Sorry Sarah, I needed to say that, but it's not how I feel. I can accept your frustration, but I think you would agree the matter is not that important, really.' Peter wondered how his daughter would respond to that kind of assessment.

She surprised him. 'No, it isn't. But I got a bad result on my science project and it hurts.'

Okay, Peter thought. He should have figured there might be a deeper reason than merely irritation. For Sarah school could be a challenge. He sat himself down next to her on the bed.

'I think I am a high achiever,' he began, taking a few seconds to gather his thoughts. 'So I know how you feel. It is difficult to face up to disappointments, or what you would call your failure right now. You are a perfectionist of sorts and that can come back to bite you. That is, if you let it.'

Sarah stared at the wall opposite and hid her surprise. Dad had never talked to her quite like that.

'Perfectionist tendencies are not wrong, but you must acknowledge to yourself that you have them and that at times they will mess with your mind.'

Sarah sat there, just listening.

'Disappointments in life are unavoidable. The worst are those in which you feel to have disappointed yourself. Well, try and learn not to let that stress you too much. Tell yourself that you can't expect to win them all and that next time you may do better. Take a deep breath.'

'It's hard,' Sarah mumbled. She felt good about this talk, more grown up somehow. She understood what her dad was saying.

'Yes, it is,' Peter said. 'Just keep telling yourself that underachievement happens but so what? Also, tell yourself, "I will try to deal with this properly. I won't overreact in my thinking." You can manage that, if you decide to.'

Sarah nodded, not sure if she would manage it, but that was okay. She would try.

Peter kept silent for a while for Sarah to mull over his advice, then gave her a hug. 'I'm proud of you,' he said. He knew that what he had suggested was far from easy but it needed saying – and repeating in future. No doubts about that.

Back in the kitchen Amelia looked concerned. 'You didn't fight with her, did you?'

'No, we talked about the difficulty of being a perfectionist. She wasn't happy with the result of her science project apparently, so she was a bit stressed out.' Amelia understood. Growing up was quite a challenge, particularly at Sarah's age. 'Is she okay? Should I go and talk to her?'

'She's fine. We had a good chat.'

'Well done, Peter.' Amelia gave him a peck on the cheek.

Peter thought he had managed a little victory, for himself and his family. It didn't feel half bad. Now where was Henry?

Reflections

- Stop, stand and think about it! Why is that so often forgotten?
- What are Peter's strong points relationally in this story?

- Had Peter made a blunder, what might have been the negative consequences?

4

Becoming understood

'So, you feel I don't listen?' Amelia sat back in her chair. They were having coffee in the local mall.

It was not the conversation Peter was looking for, but it was happening. 'Okay, you listen, but you are sometimes not prepared to see my point of view.'

'Perhaps I don't agree with it.'

'That's not really the point. You seem to disagree because you have already made up your mind that my side of the story, how I feel, is immature, or whatever, and simply shouldn't be that way.'

'And you never do that?'

'I try not to.'

They had had this discussion before. It usually ended in a stalemate, something you got over and on with.

'No, perhaps you don't,' Amelia said, 'but your

manner changes, and it's a real nuisance.' Peter could be impossible at times. Particularly on days when he was under pressure. For someone like her, who preferred the happy side of life, it was annoying. Amelia had a stubborn streak and would not take his allegation lying down.

'I know,' Peter admitted reflecting on the moods that could get hold of him. He never enjoyed being that way one little bit, but it came up from deep within and was difficult to deal with. For whatever reason, he felt he needed Amelia as an anchor in those situations. Amelia, whom he knew preferred to walk a mile away from problems. Peter didn't actually blame her for how she responded.

'More coffee?' he asked.

Amelia nodded. Peter went to order.

'Look,' he said, seated with a fresh cappuccino. 'I'm sorry. Let's forget it.'

'At times, I just don't understand you.' Amelia considered that probably she didn't want to and felt the pressure of having to, too unreasonable.

'I know. Fair enough.'

'Perhaps I fail to understand you because you seem unreasonable.'

Peter remained silent. He was not going to explain it again and let his gaze drift over the people scurrying about in the mall. He felt sad. It hadn't been a great week.

'We made a kind of pact,' Amelia said, after a while.

Peter looked at her. It would be those lectures on relating. Amelia was wonderful and he loved her. He should stop expecting her always to detect his deep-seated need patterns and to come to the party.

'Look,' Amelia continued, 'I found that place-making equation interesting and it seems true enough. We both need to learn from it.' She briefly paused and added, 'I'm sorry, if I'm stubborn sometimes, but find you difficult to fathom at times.'

'Sure.' Peter could hardly argue with that and often found it difficult himself. 'If I remember correctly, it starts with turning, with mind-set,' he suggested and left the sentence hanging in the air.

'You feel I have the wrong mind-set? How about yours?' Amelia detected an accusation and was getting fed-up with it.

'Okay, I'm sorry. Of course, it starts with mind-set. And I wasn't accusing you, just stating facts.'

I am becoming far too sensitive about it all, Amelia thought. Also, Peter was right actually. It did start with turning and she had been too annoyed to care for it. But it took two to tango. 'Well, how about your mind, Peter?'

Peter looked at his coffee – a cup half empty. 'You know that I love you, Amelia. And that I need you.' He looked at his wife. 'I don't want to make your life difficult, if I can help it.' But sometimes I do, big-time, Peter admitted to himself.

Amelia returned his gaze. Her husband was a complex man – or perhaps just a man, and they're all complex. 'We better go,' she said. 'Henry needs picking up from tennis.'

Reflections

- How is an unhelpful mood best dealt with?
- Amelia considered that 'perhaps she didn't want to understand because it was unreasonable.' How about that thought?

- If the relational dynamic of Turning were to function well, how might the story have been different?

5

The human food processor

'You don't really like cooking, mum, do you?' Henry was hovering about in the kitchen where Amelia was preparing dinner.

'No, I can't say that I do.'

'So, why can't we go out or get take-away?'

'Because I care, I'm responsible and I have to live with myself.' Not exactly the answer for a 10 year old, Amelia thought. But yes, she didn't feel like cooking, surely not today, and the conversation was beginning to push her buttons.

Henry seemed mystified, but unperturbed. 'Can I have some ice-cream?'

'No, you can't,' Amelia responded with some force. 'And don't ask why not because you know full well.'

'Why not?'

'Watch it, Henry. Don't get me cross. I suggest you go do your homework.' Her temper was rising.

'I haven't got any.'

'That's a lie, Henry.'

'Not much anyway.' Henry decided not to push his luck too far and left to play a computer game. Mum was not in a great mood.

I cook, because I care, Amelia reflected silently. And because I am responsible. And because I have to live with myself. She had spontaneously blurted it out to Henry and only now saw how true this actually was. When just married, and working full-time, she had often refused to cook. Peter very occasionally would prepare a meal or they had bought their dinners. It had been fun. Working fewer hours these days, and with a tighter budget, restaurant visits were less frequent by far. Peter always came home late so now he would only cook on weekends.

I have become a habitual cook, Amelia thought and wondered why. But she knew full well why. She was convinced of the importance of good food. This realisation had come gradually as she had read up on nutrition and felt concern about the wellbeing of her children. It hurt though that the family seemed not to appreciate it. Henry undoubtedly would prefer a less conscientious mother. Anyway, the family budget didn't allow for fast-food indulgences too often and less so since they moved into a new home.

'Is there any soft drink?' Henry ambled back in looking for a glass, having not quite made it as far as the computer before his taste buds began to demand attention.

'Have some orange juice.'

Henry opened the fridge door wide taking his time finding the bottle, then closed it with some force. Amelia managed not to speak a mild rebuke, just in time. She didn't want to be a grumpy mother.

'What's for dinner then,' Henry enquired with his mouth half into the glass of juice.

'Fish.'

Henry went back to the computer without comment.

How do I ever extract personal significance out of cooking, Amelia thought? I'm just a convenient human food processor. But she knew that was not really so. Fortunately, she understood her cooking to be an expression of love and of responsibility, however tedious it might be. In offering this service she was actually true to herself, even if she didn't like it much. As an act of caring it fitted in well with what she was learning about relational principles. Cooking for a family, however mundane an activity if you didn't feel like it, actually was relational. Even if those devouring the offerings would give that fact little thought. She would do something about that though. She might be cook, but she wasn't a doormat. Tomorrow would be take-away-day, Amelia decided, switching on the hotplate. And Peter could cook on Saturday.

Reflections

- What's the secret to caring when you don't feel like it?
- Should Peter let Amelia cook that often?
- How many other words (or work) like 'cooking' can you think of?

6

Skateboard misadventures

'But I told you before,' Amelia said angrily. 'You could have got yourself seriously hurt.' Henry began to shed some tears.

'I should put that skateboard away until you can see some sense. Look at your knee!' Henry didn't need to look. He knew full well that it hurt.

'Oh, Henry.' Amelia put her arms around him. 'Don't cry, my boy.'

But why shouldn't he. Amelia could see that he was shaken a little. It had been a close shave when he jumped off just missing that wall. She was reacting naturally, but not wisely. Why rub it in when someone is hurting?

'Sit down for a minute,' Amelia suggested, 'here with me on the bench.' Henry sat down and wiped his eyes with the back of his hand. He was not seriously injured but felt none too flash. He liked his skateboard though and would get better at it.

'When I was young I used to fall off horses,' Amelia said. 'My mum was terrified that I would break something, which I did once, a finger, but not from falling off.' Those were the days when she used to live in the country many years ago.

'Huh.' Henry wondered where this was leading.

'Just to say that I know how you feel.' And she did. Riding had been a real passion; little would have stopped her doing it. But her father would never let her mount his own horse. Leave that one for later, he had ordered. Later had never come.

Henry didn't comment.

'You like your skateboard, don't you?' Not a smart question; Amelia knew full well that Henry did. The way he looked at her clearly questioned why she was stating the obvious. 'Do you have to be that wild with it?'

Henry shrugged his shoulders. Amelia quietly rebuked herself. She was not helping her hurting son very much. His knee needed attending to, though it could wait. 'I have to try new things,' Henry said softly, but with conviction.

'Dangerous things?'

Henry nodded.

'Why?' Another quite unhelpful question. Why

indeed? But the answer was simple and revealing. It struck a chord with Amelia – with memories from days gone by.

'Because I like it.' Henry looked down at the floor tiles.

'And so you should,' Amelia commented after a moment to Henry's significant surprise. 'But don't go stupid with it.' I'm caring, she reflected. I'm trying to really understand and to be kind with it. I is so hard to let your children follow their star, even in a small way.

'My knee hurts.' Henry felt to spur his mother on to some loving attention of a more physiological kind.

'I'll clean it up in a minute, but first I have a suggestion.'

Henry gave his mum a careful look.

'You should talk to dad and see how you might take that skateboarding further without hurting yourself unnecessarily.'

'It may cost,' replied Henry after a while, ever the opportunist.

Amelia smiled at her son who was so much like his mother. 'I know,' she said. 'Come on, let's get that knee sorted.'

Reflections

- What should I watch out for when reacting from a perspective of 'what might have happened!'?
- How do you know you are connecting at a feeling level?
- What reasons can you find that Amelia dealt with the situation competently?

7

Just a little garden job

Sarah was not happy. She had arranged with Kylie to stay for the night and needed a lift. 'How can I get there if you don't take me?' she accused her father. 'Why won't you?' She stood looking intently at Peter, who sat in a chair opposite.

'I don't feel like it, actually. I've done my bit for the day.' Peter put his head back behind the newspaper he was reading.

'Mum, tell Dad not to be so impossible.' Sarah looked pleadingly at her mother who seemed to show little interest. 'You take me, Mum?'

'No. Sorry Sarah, taxi driving is your father's business in the evenings.' Amelia seemed unperturbed about her daughter's plight. She had an idea what this was really about.

'Tell me,' Peter asked Sarah, 'what makes you think that I should just get up for a half hour's drive when I have been on the road enough today?'

'Because, you're my father,' Sarah blurted out in annoyance.

'Sure, but why should I be responsible?'

'I don't know Dad, but you are. I can always trust you to drop me off somewhere. You are never difficult about it. So why now?'

'Why should I be trustworthy, if you are not?' The question stopped Sarah in her tracks. This was becoming personal in a way she had not foreseen.

'What do you mean?'

'Five days ago you promised to rake up the leaves in the garden within two days. It hasn't been done.'

The light dawned with Sarah. 'I'll do it over the weekend,' she promised.

'Then I will take you to Kylie next week,' Peter answered.

'Come on Dad, it's only a few leaves.' Sarah was getting worried. Her father was not usually like that. Perhaps, Mum was behind it all.

'If it is only a few leaves, I see no reason why you couldn't keep to the agreement. It isn't much work. I agree.' Peter seemed determined to stick to his guns. In truth, he didn't feel like driving to Kylie's.

Sarah was lost for words and felt like storming out of the room. But that would close the door on a lift for sure. 'Come on, Dad,' she pleaded.

'Do you think it is unreasonable of me not to fulfil my driving duties in this family, if you don't stick to the garden deal? Why should I be any different from you? And don't say because I'm older. That garden job is dead easy. You could have done it.'

'I don't know.'

'So, you want me to be responsible, but yourself, you don't have to be?' Peter sought to drive the point home for the benefit of his daughter.

Sarah sat down. Words were drying up. She also realised that she would get to Kylie okay after this was resolved. Unless she was going to be stubborn about it. Dad had a point.

'So?' Peter asked.

'Yes, okay Dad, you're right.'

'That's not good enough Sarah.'

'I'm sorry, Dad.'

'Listen Sarah, it's quite simple. If you cannot be responsible in little things now, how can you be so later on in the bigger ones? And if you can't do that, and life is full of those responsibilities, you're facing an unhappy future.' Peter imagined this advice to be water on a duck's back, but it needed to be said.

Sarah no longer felt like saying much.

'Okay, let's consider it behind us,' Peter decided. 'But next time I won't budge that easily.'

'Thanks, Dad.'

'Go get your bag, honey.' Peter was getting up out of his chair. Amelia purposefully didn't look at either of them. But she was pleased.

Reflections

- 'Why should I be trustworthy, when you are not?' Peter asks. Well, why should he?

- If the few leaves were mine to clear and I didn't, what would that show?
- What, really, made Peter become a driver after all?

8

The cost of a bargain

'Where does this come from?' Amelia wanted to know holding up a book about vintage cars.

'From the shop,' Peter responded curtly. 'Was a bargain.'

'Never mind bargains. We agreed you would not buy any more of those books for a while, as you have plenty already.' It was true. They had agreed on that. 'Also, you were hiding it, in your office.'

'It wasn't hiding,' Peter defended himself, being on the back foot. 'And how about that new perfume you bought recently? Isn't that rather expensive?''

If looks could kill, at that moment Amelia would have been a murderer. 'I saved it from my house-keeping.'

'So, that's all right then. The housekeeping does not belong to you, but to our family. I will save the cost of the book from my petrol money by not being a family taxi anymore for a while.' This isn't helping, Peter reflected. And indeed, it was horrible. 'Sorry,' he offered. 'I shouldn't have said that.'

'I never promised not to save from the household budget. But you did promise to stop buying those books.' Amelia was not easily cowered. Her temper, once up, could flatten mountains.

Peter sighed. It was fair enough. He had well and truly blown it.

'You should practise what you preach,' Amelia commented angrily.

'What do you mean?'

'You're all for openness with each other, and that sort of stuff, as long as it suits. You say you value me, but then you play me this trick.'

'I do value you,' Peter objected.

'But not so much that you could resist buying this book and hiding it?' Amelia, having made her point walked out of the room into the passageway. Peter followed.

'Okay, I was wrong,' he admitted. 'I agree, it was a stupid thing to do.'

Amelia turned towards him. 'Now, why exactly was it stupid?'

Momentarily, Peter was taken aback. It was a penetrating question. Not one to answer glibly. He gave it thought while Amelia waited with expectation.

'I let you down and it undermines your trust in me,' Peter finally confessed.

'Yes, you did.' Amelia was beginning to lose her anger and for an instant felt strangely vulnerable.

Peter noticed. 'I'm sorry,' he said, and meant it. 'It won't happen again.'

Amelia stood quite still and after a while said, 'Fine. Accepted.' Then, she added, 'And I won't save for myself out of the family budget anymore.'

'It was a rotten thing to say,' Peter admitted contritely. He disliked himself for that unreasonable and too convenient comment. Amelia deserved better. 'Why don't we increase our personal allowances?'

'I don't want to talk about that now,' Amelia responded. 'You can make me a coffee, if you like.' The topic was closed.

While filling up the kettle Peter reflected that he had been a fool. If he really wanted that book so badly, he should have discussed it. More allowance seemed a good idea. Amelia was not often unreasonable and when she seemed to be, she was usually right. He had done some damage and was determined to make up for it in future. He considered Amelia and himself to be close as a couple and badly wished to keep it that way.

Reflections

- What is the relational message inherent in Peter's behaviour?
- What might have been the reasons for his initial response?
- What is the potential damage done?

9

What if?

'I'd box his ears,' Peter declared playfully.

'No, you won't.' Peter never used violence in anything. 'Just try to be serious for a moment,' Amelia warned. They were sitting together on the couch with the TV on mute.

'Perhaps you could switch the TV off for a while,' Amelia suggested. 'I'll read this case study out again and this time please listen.'

'I've heard it.' Peter said.

'Just listen.'

'You are asked to make an appointment with the school principal as your child has fallen out with a teacher and there could be significant repercussions. You are aware that the child has difficulties with that particular teacher. Interpret this situation and apply *Living Well* principles.'

'Okay,' Amelia suggested. 'Let's take the three principles, one at a time.'

That was fine with Peter. Matter of fact, he was beginning to value the wisdom of what they were learning. 'I'd start with my child,' he suggested. 'Find out what the real problem is. And, as the situation is not new, I probably would have some idea already.'

'But you won't be reactionary?'

'Definitely not.'

'Yes. That sounds like a caring approach.'

The next point was the responsibility factor.

Amelia said, 'I would consider whether we had given the situation enough attention in the past. Had we really owned the problem as parents, or just paid lip service to it.'

'Excellent.' Peter commented. It sounded like his work environment.

'So, how would you approach the harmony factor?' Amelia asked Peter.

'I would try to be fair to all parties concerned. No chips on shoulders.'

'But say you don't like that teacher?'

'Possible.' Peter admitted. There had been a few people in his life like that. He decided to return the question. 'How would *you* take a responsible approach with a teacher you dislike?' he asked.

'Try to listen to the teacher with an open mind, but not taking the information without comment. And if there is anything the teacher says that seems fair enough we deal with it.'

'That then also addresses the harmony aspect,' Peter said. 'Seeing it from the teacher's perspective. But, what if you feel your child is being provoked?'

'Then, I'll say so.' And surely she would, Amelia thought. 'I'd also discuss it with the school Principal.'

'Not an easy job that, being Principal.' Peter would never wish to be one. Too many parties to keep happy. It would drive him 'round the bend. Parents, teachers, volunteers and the government. And not to forget the pupils.

'Yes, I accept that,' Amelia agreed. 'But having accepted the job it comes with its responsibilities.'

'Now you're talking,' Peter replied somewhat tongue in cheek. 'You're getting good at this stuff.'

'Shut up Peter. Be serious.'

Amelia had commented about responsibilities spontaneously and not really as a result of the *Living Well* sessions. It was quite an obvious observation. But it showed how true to life this relational information actually was.

'Sure.' Peter felt they had covered the basics. 'I think we're getting the hang of this.'

'Absolutely,' Amelia responded dryly. 'Until the situation really occurs.'

'Then, we'll see again,' Peter grinned. 'I'm sure you will do brilliantly, honey.' He actually believed that to be true.

'As if,' Amelia commented. 'And don't leave me carrying the candle, when troubles come.'

Amelia well knew Peter would never do so. Fortunately, Sarah was no bother at school. Henry was a different story. She might do right in giving it more attention.

'Could you pass me the remote, please?' Peter asked with one eye on the TV.

This urgency of getting their discussion ended annoyed Amelia a little. 'Get it yourself,' she said and walked to the kitchen to check on what was available for Sarah and Henry to make their school lunches in the morning.

Reflections

- Amelia and Peter discuss an acceptable approach to the problem. What would the wrong approach look like?
- Briefly consider the possible difficulties arising from a negative relational attitude.
- If the teacher has a valid point then what, and how?

10

Game troubles

'I need to get to the shop for that Play Station game,' Henry told his father.

'Not my problem,' Peter responded. He was working in his office on a report that needed tabling at work tomorrow. 'Go, ask your mother.'

'She's off to the book club. Got no time. She told me to ask you.' Clearly, Henry was less than impressed and felt a little helpless. He had looked forward to getting this new game today.

'Neither have I got time. Your mum knows I'm busy.' Peter was becoming irritated and it showed.

'But I booked that game over a week ago,' Henry objected in desperation. 'And mum promised then she would take me – and now she isn't.'

Peter got up from behind his desk. This needed sorting. 'I'll go and talk to your mother,' he said.

He found Amelia scanning through the book she was to present that evening. 'What's this about a video game,' Peter asked none too friendly.

'Henry booked it, and I forgot about the book club,' Amelia explained. 'I have no time to pick it up.'

'You promised, so you can't just walk away from that,' Peter countered.

'Oh, here's mister perfect speaking, who always is so well organised.' Amelia got her hackles up from Peter's attitude.

'Look,' he said, 'I've got no time either.'

Amelia walked to the kitchen to get her car keys. 'Fair enough, then Henry will have to learn to wait.' She made for the back door.

Henry, who had followed the interaction over a distance, was near to tears. 'That's not fair,' he objected loudly. 'If we don't pick up that game today, it'll be gone.'

Peter stood exasperated in the kitchen. His son was leaving for his room and a bed to cry on, while his wife was angry. His concentration had been shattered and the report would be ten times more difficult to write. What a mess! He needed a coffee, and put the kettle on.

Henry, appearing from behind the kitchen door, had decided to broach the topic one final time. 'Dad?' he said not so loudly.

'Come through, son. It's not your fault.' Peter felt

for his little fellow. He didn't look at Henry and concentrated on pouring hot water. 'We'll get that game together.'

'Mum shouldn't have forgotten,' Henry offered.

Peter looked at him. 'She shouldn't have, but she did. None of us are that fool-proof.'

Henry wisely shut up and accepted a cookie from the jar his dad presented.

Peter reflected ruefully how easily a small matter could blow up into considerable difficulties. Because he had reacted unwisely, concentrating too much on that report. It'd better be a good game. Henry had had his eyes on it for a while now.

'Come on, champ.' Peter lifted young Henry up against his chest in a bear hug heading for the car. 'I might play that game with you.'

Reflections

- Which of the six *Living Well* relational principles can you find in this story?
- Who dealt better with the situation, Peter or Amelia, and why?

• Amelia forgot but she was welcome to, Peter explained to Henry. What does that show?

11

A matter of trust

Peter sat slumped in his favourite chair and looked exhausted.

'You're simply working too hard,' Amelia said, 'Haven't you achieved enough this year?'

'I've got a target in mind that can be reached,' he grumbled in response.

'Yes, and I bet it's more than is expected,' Amelia observed ruefully. 'Success is just so important to you, isn't it?'

'Don't knock it, babe.' Peter was on the defensive now. He felt spent, but a night's sleep should fix it.

'No. I appreciate how hard you work, but for what? Is it going to pay you so much more?' Amelia knew her husband only too well. She realised that she should let him achieve, that was what made him tick after all. But she knew the downside of it and was worried about its possible repercussions.

'It'll bring a bonus,' Peter mumbled.

'Yes, but at what cost?' Amelia was determined to stay reasonable and made sure not to put tension in her voice. 'I mean, it doesn't do you much good, Peter.' Nor our family, she thought.

Peter didn't respond. He had been wondering lately whether his life was getting out of balance. It surely felt that way. Why did he always have to be one of the best operators in the company?

Amelia seemed to read his mind. 'What is it that tells you to push yourself that hard?' she asked. She knew that Peter was not always as confident as he projected.

'You really want to know?' Peter regretted the question immediately. And then he didn't. Perhaps it was time to talk.

'Yes Peter, I would - if you don't mind telling.'

Peter hesitated. He was now facing a significant moment. A turning point somehow. It was time to trust his wife. 'Can I trust you?' he asked. But of course he could.

Amelia remained silent for a while looking at

Peter. 'Yes,' she said and meant it. This would not be information that was to be bounced back at him later for whatever reason.

Her simple 'Yes' dismantled any barrier Peter might have felt. 'I like being positive and efficient,' he explained, 'and I fear failure. Not enormously, but I do.'

The confession hung in the air. Amelia let it settle and was not that surprised. She had figured it out over the years anyway. But it would be good to discuss it openly. After some thought she said, 'And you are afraid that actually you will fail?'

'No, not really. At least, not yet. But I could overreach one day. Perhaps that day is coming closer?' Peter straightened up a little in his chair.

Amelia felt for her husband. It was a tough world out there in commerce. Her job, three days a week, had hassles enough. Still, she thought he should know better and said, 'You've got it all wrong, Peter. You have long proven what you are capable of. It's time to get the monkey off your back.'

'What monkey?'

'The one that climbed on years ago. As a capable

young man you would have discovered that people praised you when you were achieving. You liked success and it gave you identity. It became your way of coping effectively with life. Also, you like people, and that altogether is a very potent mix for excellent performances. But it's a trap, unless you draw the line and get on top of this need for continual recognition.' Amelia spoke with feeling. She knew that she was right and was wondering about her own continual need of feeling happy and untroubled. Balance in life didn't come easily, emotionally or otherwise.

'You're right,' Peter admitted after some time, being quietly surprised at the insight of his wife. 'We should talk about it some more, but I'm too tired for that right now.'

'Why don't we go away for a weekend?' Amelia suggested. She had wanted to do that soon anyway – to touch base together. 'Your mother might be willing to have Sarah and Henry.'

'Weekend after next,' Peter concluded without hesitation. In the meantime he would begin to reflect more on his lifestyle overall, what drove him and why? Was success really the measure of his identity?

Reflections

- How might the *Living Well* relational principles help against overworking?
- Leaving my vulnerabilities unmentioned in a close relationship is unwise. Why might this be so?
- Why will many people never open up about it, not even to themselves?

12

It's a deal

Amelia and Peter sat on the veranda of a country cottage which they had rented for a weekend. It was dusk with orange colours lacing the blue sky where the sun hit streaks of cloud. It had been a good few days, relaxing and profitable. They had not felt that close to each other for a long time. Both had taken care in being sensitive listeners without immediate answers or opinions. If not a watershed, it was at least an important step forward relationally. For too long matters in family life had been left to roll on, one after the other, without sufficient evaluation. There was always the next issue or activity that clambered for attention. Touching base was no longer taking place much. Intuitively Peter and Amelia felt that this cycle needed breaking. It had been the reason for Amelia enrolling them in those sessions on relating.

Peter was encouraged by his wife not making light of his identity struggles involving success. She took it seriously – not as a problem, but as a matter that needed attention towards a personally more liberating perspective. With Amelia positively in support half the battle would be won.

Amelia in turn had shared that many of her smiles actually concealed a considerable sadness. The world was a mess with many people suffering. It pained her and her response usually was to think of something happy instead. Peter did not think this silly and had encouraged her in coming out from behind the "happy" façade. To Amelia his understanding had been nothing less than a blessing. Peter seemed glad to discuss her dilemma. Occasionally in the past, he had made comment about how her light-heartedness was not always lining up with how she really felt. But it was never talked through like today. Both sensed that by giving emotional space to each other they were strengthening the bond of belonging together. A bit of place-making, Amelia reflected.

'It's not just about us,' Peter commented, 'it's also the children.' The sun was noticeably dropping down behind the horizon and soon would disappear. The apparent speed at the final moments always surprised Peter.

'Yes,' Amelia agreed, 'but that starts with each of us and both of us together as well.'

Peter didn't respond.

'I think, we should be mindful of the positive relational motivators and simply tell each other when we are busy demoralising. No blame,' Amelia offered. It seemed the most obvious and best way forward.

'Well, we can try, for sure,' Peter said. 'It's a bit to remember, that model.'

Amelia detected a cop-out, though not perhaps intentionally. 'You can remember a lot of data for your job Peter, so memorising a few basics about relating shouldn't be overly difficult'

'And if I forget, I'm sure you'll keep me honest,'

Peter grinned. He loved his wife, and his children, and had already decided to make sure that those basics would become habitual, firmly embedded in his mind.

'Is this a deal, or just a good idea?' Amelia asked. So many resolutions came to nothing unless worked at.

'It's a deal, as long as the whole dynamic remains positive,' Peter suggested.

'It must,' Amelia agreed.

'And if I do well, you will acknowledge that at times?' Peter suggested

'I will, but vice versa,' Amelia challenged her husband. 'Don't you forget the deal!' These ideas could become swamped by everyday busyness too readily.

'No, I won't,' Peter promised. 'It's a deal.' Those words fleetingly reminded him of work.

Amelia extended her hand. 'Shake hands.'

'Sure.' But Peter stood up first. Taking Amelia's hand he pulled her up unto her feet. 'Time for the restaurant,' he suggested, leaving his plans for later unmentioned!

Reflections

- How can someone become a sensitive listener without ready answers?
- Describe the cycle Amelia and Peter needed to break.
- How would you proceed in becoming relationally competent?